© Laura Levine 1983

KENNEDYS

THE UNAUTHORIZED VERSION

Edited by f-Stop Fitzgerald • Written by Marian Kester

Dedication:

to John Fitzgerald Kennedy,
whose assassination
marred my fourteenth birthday celebration
and royally screwed up the nation.

—f-Stop Fitzgerald
(b. November 22, 1949)

The Magic Bullet

The bullet which, after passing through the President's throat, stopping dead in midair, turning at a sharp angle, shattering Governor Connally's fifth rib, then his wrist, and finally entering his thigh, was somehow "discovered" lying on a stretcher (whether JFK's or Connally's, no one knows) at Parkland Hospital in virtually unscathed condition. The bullet was planted there in all likelihood because it had been fired from the rifle that Kennedy's assassins had assigned to be the "murder weapon." (See Mark Lane, *Rush to Judgement*, 1966)

© Target Video 1983

MAGIC BULLET MUSIC

"Dead Kennedys" is a great name not only in the sense "Sex Pistols" is a great name because it is inspired violence of condensed language, but because it is rooted in a crucial subconscious realization: the Kennedys are dead, goddammit—who killed them and why? Who's running this show? Who wants to die for a country that's already dead? Who wants to *live* in one? Lead singer Jello Biafra was only four in 1963 but his memory, fortunately, is longer than his biological time-span. And isn't this what's central to the most horrifying science fiction scenarios: that people *forget* what life was like before 1984, before the Brave New World, before Nightfall, before Soylent Green, before Rollerball? The little light of "eternal vigilance" is extinguished, and no power on earth can ever fire it up again. . .

The Kennedy Brothers, indigenous dynasty, crown princes, our twilight triumvirate ruling by divine right. It's amusing to think of the early 60s as America's Camelot; that means the 50s must have been the Garden of Eden. Everything's relative, though, as far as we know so far, so why not make the Pentagon a Round Table and Lee Harvey Oswald a Mordred and the whole era a nostalgic sentimental favorite? Nothing better illustrates the innate monarchism of the masses, given half a chance, than this phenomenon: that America, nation of No Class, home of "More" and "Success is its own reward," land of leveling and inorganic polymer clothing for all, capital of Casual, should have its Kennedys. And, perhaps to appease the powers of darkness below that balance our trite lit-up world on their glistening black backs, we have our Dead Kennedys as well.

Well, in the long view, of course, the early 60s looks less like Arthurian legend and more like pale lipstick, the Beatles in Hamburg, the Peace Corps, the Port Huron Statement, dear old Khrushchev warts and all, James Bond, "Bye Bye Birdie," minis and Cape Canaveral. And it felt a lot less epic when you were *there*. But the trouble with "the long view" is that it can reduce damn near everything to so much shit, which may prompt you to go kill yourself if you're not careful. Taking the short view is usually tons more fun. (Although you pay handsomely for it in the end, ha ha, just as the Presbyterians thought. How else could there be a book about. . .

the Dead Kennedys.

[Our name] was meant to call attention to the beginnings of the "Me Generation" which started with the Kennedy assassinations, because the Kennedy assassinations torpedoed the American Dream. "America growing bigger, better! Out in space! Bigger cars! Movie star President and his gorgeous wife!" Kaboom! The balance tilts. And it tilted slowly, but where are we now?

(Biafra interviewed by George Ypsilantis, *BAM*, 4/10/81)

Back to the original, live Kennedys, briefly. Even Jacqueline, once married—rather uneasily—to a Brother, will remain forever royal in our eyes. Even Marilyn dons a posthumous crown for her association with a Brother or Brothers. No one doubts for an instant that Jack would have been re-elected in '64, that Bobby would have won handily in '68, or that Teddy could have the Presidency any time if he really wanted it. Trying to find out what Teddy *really* wants is something of a national pastime, and in election years becomes the entirety of Democratic Party politics; this will hardly end even with the great non-event of 1982, "Teddy Won't Run, He Says."

Nothing short of assassination can suffice to deprive us of a Kennedy. It is the only way a Kennedy—ordinarily deathless—may become "dead." And it is here that the roots of the fixed fascination with Kennedys really lie. You don't simply knock off a nation's major symbolic public figure—twice!—and then call it "just one of those things," without throwing that nation's development and public life way, way off. Carl Oglesby is one who was there back in the early 60s, active in SDS (Students for a Democratic Society—which is exactly what they were), and who believes that JFK was assassinated by a militarist wing of the American ruling class (the Cowboys) in concert with the CIA and Mafia.

We're well-trained by the CIA
With Yankee tax money in Ft. Bragg
The Peace Corps builds us labor camps
When they think they're building schools

When Cowboy Ronnie comes to town
Forks out his tongue at human rights...

(*Bleed For Me*, words and music by Biafra, Ray, Flouride, Peligro, © 1982 Decay Music)

In his book *The Yankee and Cowboy War* (1976), Oglesby argues that America cannot proceed one step further forward in history until we indeed come to grips with this fact: we are run by clandestine powers which engage in intrigue against the people and against one another: "a multitude of conspiracies contend in the night." What could be more un-American? In the modern U.S.:

> Conspiracy is the normal continuation of normal politics by normal means...But to get at Dallas '63 would be to get at this sickness by one of its major victories. It would be to get at the political bottom of the Vietnam war, of the structures of internal conflict that helped produce the entire decade, the decade of Dallas-Watergate and Vietnam. Understand Dallas: that is the start of the way out...*If we cannot say who killed the president, then there is no respect in which we may still see ourselves as a self-governing people.* (Emphasis added.)

Well before Oglesby, the journalist Thomas Buchanan stated flatly in *Who Killed Kennedy?* (1964) this same idea that in murdering JFK, his political assassins tried to deal a death-blow to the democratic spirit itself:

> I do not believe this case is closed. I do not think it will be, until some more satisfying answer has been given to the question which aroused the world: Why was the President of the United States assassinated? I believe we do his memory no service in pretending no one but a lonely madman could have wished him dead. If this were so, his death would have no meaning. I believe he lived for something, and I think he died for something. Any man is measured by his enemies. The list of those who hated Kennedy the day he died does honor to him. It must never be forgotten that he went to Dallas to combat these men, to tell the people of that city, of the nation and the world beyond that peace was not a sign of weakness.
> Neither is ability to face the truth a sign of weakness. It would be interpreted, throughout the world, as evidence of the maturity of the United States. For we are not dishonored as a nation by attempts to find the murderers among us, but by our attempts to hide them.
> It is not the light we must fear; it is the darkness.

(This book has been 'out of print' since the year it was published; it has, however, been translated into 18 languages and is still in print in Europe. No wonder Europeans know more about American history than we do.)

Melodramatic stuff. It's fashionable now to discount JFK's presidency as "lackluster" and "mediocre," just as it's fashionable to see the 50s as an age of warped rebellion seething just beneath the bland surface, as if everybody's dad spent the decade hotly refusing to testify before HUAC. But such opinion-fads hardly matter. The injury has been suffered, the outrage has been committed, the innocence has been ruptured. What matters is that *we feel it to be so*, in spite of ourselves. And buried in our gut feeling is the clandestine truth of those assassinations—for insult was added to injury with the elimination of RFK as well—a truth which as the years go by escapes into more and more inaccessible cracks in the facade of American life.

Lest we forget, then...

the Dead Kennedys.

Accepting an award from the California record industry, 1980—Klaus, Biafra, Ray and former drummer Bruce Slesinger.

The Dead Kennedys are much more than this year's political gimmick joke band. They are more than the Eighties' answer to Country Joe and the Fish. In fact they might be one of the most important bands to come out of this scene.

(*Slash*, L.A., October 1979)

© Winston Smith 1983

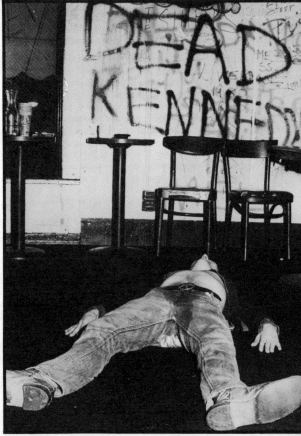

Biafra

Drug me with natural vitamin C
Drug me with pharmaceutical speed
Drug me with your sleeping pills
Drug me with your crossword puzzles
Drug me with your magazines
Drug me with your fuck machines
With a fountain of fads
More rock and roll ads
DRUG ME DRUG ME DRUG ME

(*Drug Me*, words and music by Biafra, © 1980 Decay Music)

Elite Club, San Francisco, 1981

© Gary Robert 1983

© Sue Brisk 1983

Born to play drums.

DEAD KENNEDYS

OLD WALDORF
OCTOBER 25   8 PM

Poster for Old Waldorf, artist unknown

For the first time we can actually know what Jello is singing. This is quite revealing. He's seething and reeking with new and different political suggestions, and responsible for a most bizarre, though not unreasonable, platform. For example: Now that the U.S. is technically so far advanced, why not solve a large part of our economic problem by disintegrating slums with the neutron bomb ("Kill the Poor")?

(review by patirl [sic] in *Ripper,* Santa Cruz, 1980)

Bruce Slesinger (left) left the band because of "musical differences." (Klaus on right)

© Sue Brisk 1983

---------------------------------- GUITAR (CONTINUED FROM P. 1)------------- G

(CONT. FROM P. 1)   INTERESTED IN COLLABORATING W/ SOME ACCOMPLISHED SONGWRITERS.   74G

NAME: MARC   SF   75G*
ACOUSTIC GUITAR PLAYER/SINGER/SONGWRITER, 5YRS, SEEKS SAME TO FORM DUO DOING COPY &
ORIGINALS. HAVE GIGS AND REHEARSAL PLACE.

NAME: MARC   SF   75G*
GUITAR PLAYER/SINGER/SONGWRITER: 5YRS. WANTS TO JAM & FORM BAND W/ OTHER MUSICIANS.
ORIGINALS AND LOTS OF ROCK N' ROLL. HAVE REHEARSAL PLACE & POSSIBLE GIGS.

NAME: RAY   OAKLAND   58G*
GUITAR, 6 YRS. HAS FINANCIAL BACKING. WANTS LEAD SINGER, KEYBD, BASS, DRUMS, OR A
BAND FOR NEW WAVE/PUNK.

NAME: LARRY AUSTIN   PHONE: 76G*
AVAILABLE...ROCK GUITARIST
DEMOS &

NAME: 21G*
GUIT
NO T4

NAME: 31G*
GUITAR

NAME: 77G*
LD GUIT
SEEKS:

----   XXX

SEE...
...and 2

                                                                                  100

NAME: 126
BAND CURR
SEEK: RE

NAME: 125
T40/DISCO.   SACRAMENTO.
SEEK: GUI

NAME: SF   124
3 VOC'S & A RHYT GUIT SEEK: LD GUIT, DRUMMER, & BASS.

NAME: SF   123
SOUL, DISCO, MOR, T40: T40 BAND ALREADY WORKING AS A TRIO SEEKS: FEM VOC/GUIT OR
FEM VOC/HORN, OR ANY PRO FRONT PERSON (M OR F) VOC/INSTRUMENT.

NAME: WALTER OR JOHNNY   SF   118*
"LINN COUNTY": NAME GOES BACK TO 60'S, PRESENT MEMBERS TOGETHER 3 YRS. LD VOC (14YRS
EXP), DRUM (10YRS), ORGAN (10YRS). OLD R&B & SOUL, SOME BLUES. HAVE BOOKING AGENTS.
SEEK: GUIT, ELEC BASS, & SAX: ALL MUST SING HARMONY, BE ABLE TO TRAVEL, & BE
EXPERIENCED PROS.

© Lynda Burdick 1983

East Bay Ray

Klaus Flouride

DKs A TO B

Jello Biafra's real name is a secret *we'll* never tell. And yes, he's married—sorry, girls. Maybe the wedding was just a publicity stunt. Maybe it was just an excuse to wear a top hat and tails. We'll never tell and could never guess.

Drummer D.H. (Darren) Peligro doesn't operate under his real name either. The band once had a fifth member who played guitar and was known only as 6025. Klaus Flouride (bass) may well be pseudonymous. East Bay Ray (guitar) cops only to his humble origins in Castro Valley east of San Francisco. Actually all four of them are humble guys who could easily be from your hometown. Really, they might be. Klaus hails from Detroit, Peligro from East St. Louis, and Jello from Boulder, Colorado.

Biafra once told a reporter that he left Boulder at 19 because it was becoming "a haven for rich cokeheads," "an organic resort town" (Mark Leach in *Shades,* Toronto, Dec. 1981). This experience made him a "rabid environmentalist." Exactly two and one half months at UC Santa Cruz made him contemptous of hippies, and—*voilà.* In 1978 Biafra arrived in San Francisco just in time to answer an ad placed by Ray: the proverbial "Guitarist wants to start punk band."

"I have loved garage rock since I was 7 years old, and I'll always love it. It's just something in my blood," Biafra told George (Epileptic) Ypsilantis (*BAM,* op.cit.), and that was a good thing, since the Dead Kennedys were pretty fresh out of the garage when they landed their premiere gig at the Mabuhay Gardens in July 1978. The Mab was the first venue to regularly feature punk acts (unnatural as they are), a fact all those aware of the S.F. scene know well. (See Belsito and Davis, *Hardcore California: Street Level Rock and Beyond*, Last Gasp, 1983, for the whole sordid story.) By the summer of '78 there was already competition for a limited number of gigs among such bands as the Dils, Crime, the Mutants, the Avengers, and the Nuns. Then, as if a certain critical mass had been achieved, the lid blew off. Venues opened by the dozen, bands sprang up by the score. And by the time Jello Biafra ran for mayor in 1979, the Dead Kennedys were the #1 punk attraction in town.

Jello Biafra

Darren Peligro

9

Quaint Old-Fashioned Nineteenth-Century Notions

It is not "pity" that opens the gates to the most distant and strange types of being and culture to *us*, but rather our lack of partiality that does *not* empathize with or share suffering, but on the contrary takes delight in a hundred things that formerly led people to suffer (feel outraged or deeply moved). Suffering in all its nuances has become interesting for us. . .In this *voluntary* desire to contemplate all sorts of distress and transgressions, we have become stronger and more vigorous.

Modern pessimism is an expression of the uselessness of the *modern* world—not of the world of existence.

Principles have become ridiculous; nobody permits himself any longer to speak without irony of his "duty". . .We hate pompous and hieratical manners, we delight in what is most forbidden, we should hardly have any interest in knowledge if the path to it were paved with boredom. . .We consider passion a privilege, we consider nothing great unless it includes a great crime. . .We no longer love nature on account of its "innocence" or "reason" or "beauty"; we have made it nicely "devilish" and "dumb." But instead of despising it on that account, we have felt more closely related to it ever since, more at home in it. Nature does not *aspire* to virtue, and for that we respect it. . .We do not demand beautiful illusory lies from art—brutal positivism reigns, recognizing facts without becoming excited.

"Mankind" does not advance; it does not even exist.

(selections dated 1887-88 from Friedrich Nietzsche, *The Will to Power*)

11

**Biafra dictates absolutely from the stage,
secure in his ability to possess.**

A beer can bounced off the head of Biafra and he scarcely seemed to notice. Ray ducked another can that whizzed by his ear. Biafra paid scant attention to the unruly throng, crouching, bobbing and weaving, rolling on the floor and generally acting like a wild animal as he snarled out lyrics to songs like "California Uber Alles."

"I'll give you head for a couple drinks," said one inebriated young lady dressed in basic black. "I'm a fucking debutante and these are real pearls," she added, fingering her necklace.

Such is the ritual of punk rock, a burgeoning genre of primitive sounds. . .

(Joel Selvin in the *S.F. Chronicle*, October 8, 1979)

Jerry Gardner 1983

13

I am Governor Jerry Brown
My aura smiles
And never frowns
Soon I will be president. . . .
Carter power will soon go away
I will be Fuhrer one day
I will command all of you
Your kids will meditate in school
California Uber Alles
Uber Alles California
Zen Facists will control you
100% natural
You will jog for the master race
And always wear a happy face
Close your eyes, can't happen here
Big Bro' on white horse is near
The hippies won't come back you say
Mellow out or you will pay
California Uber Alles
Uber Alles California

(*California Uber Alles*, words by Biafra & John Greenway,
music by Biafra, © 1979 Decay Music)

Jerry Brown, by the way, has a copy of "California Uber Alles." I found out. He was sitting at the Savoy Tivoli in North Beach with some friends, and Jim Carroll saw him and said, "Oh hi, I'm going to run across the street and get you something." So he hops over to Recycled Records, pulls out "Uber Alles," goes back and hands it to Jerry. Brown is probably the kind of guy who'll take it home and give it a listen.

(Biafra interviewed in *Wet* by Stephen Rodefer
sometime in 1980   )

If there weren't people unafraid to be judged insane by their peers, we'd still be living in caves.

—Biafra

BIAFRA FOR MAYOR OF SAN FRANCISCO?

Punk detests all that is Hippie. But all that is 60s is not Flower Child: remember the New Left? One of the biggest, most colorful outbursts of radicalism in American history, deceased for just over a decade? Bands like the DKs, MDC, Red Crayola, Rank & File, Black Flag, T.S.O.L., Arsenal, DEVO, Fear, and D.O.A. help keep alive the bizarre, hard-won, home-grown heritage of radicalized youth. Cynical ex-leftists like to sneer at Punk politics in terms of "It's all been thought/felt/said/done before (on a much higher theoretical level)," just as superannuated teen rebels like to condescendingly point out that they, too, revolted in their youth ("with a lot more style"). Punks say So What. Such remarks don't even address the question, the one burning question of each fresh generation: WHAT IS TO BE DONE? Every generation must act for itself. Bedtime stories about what our betters (elders) did when *they* were young and warlike just don't make it.

1979, only in San Francisco. What matter that he was underage, or that he ran, contrary to law, under a false name? Biafra's campaign for Mayor was fair play in a city which plans to release Dan White, the assassin of its former mayor, after a term of less than 5 years; a city which currently features a female mayor who passionately believes only criminals should retain the right to carry handguns. Frisco, superficially harmonious, is in fact deeply polarized; each faction (homosexuals, families, feminists, prostitutes, cops, landlords, the poor, winos, Chicanos, Asians, blacks, whites, ecology freaks, etc.) has its own candidate; and if things haven't gotten really nasty yet, it's only because Frisco has a long tradition of limp handshakes to overcome before it can take up fisticuffs.

So what was the Punk Program for San Francisco? Here again the DKs unfurled the furtive banner of 60's radicalism: like SDS before him, Biafra merely *took seriously* America's self-image as liberal paradise with opportunity for all. Whenever these pieties are taken literally, all hell breaks loose. Much of Biafra's "platform" was just whimsical: "clean up Market Street" by requiring businessmen to wear clownsuits from 9 to 5, have a Board of Bribery to set "influence" rates, hire laid-off city workers to panhandle money for the city coffers, erect Dan White statues for the citizenry to throw rotten eggs at. Other planks of the platform were just liberal common sense: rent control, public works programs, fixing standard rates for city services, electing police, imposing bans on auto use downtown and on construction of more skyscrapers. But as such it could not have been more utopian.

A noticeable fraction of the populace voted for this last hope, or last straw, despite the expenditure of a mere $1500 on his campaign and a slogan that went "Apocalypse Now! Vote Biafra." Tony Rocco, social observer/participant, wrote at the time that

> Hopeless idealists and hardened cynics from punks to high school teachers saw that in him they had at least a meaningful protest vote and possibly a chance to make a statement that wouldn't be ignored by the media.

(*Damage* #4, December 1979)

No, the media did not exactly ignore the hopeless idealism and hardened cynicism of 4% of the voters who in giving Biafra 6,591 of their votes made him fourth in a field of ten candidates. There's always room for Jello. . .But barely room enough for the two major candidates, who were forced into a runoff since the punk spoiler had deprived either of a majority.

By way of explaining his triumph, Biafra crowed, "Anyone can rob a bank. Anyone can draw a picture." And in America, anyone can make an impression on the bored electorate without half trying.

Campaign buttons by Ephemera © 1979

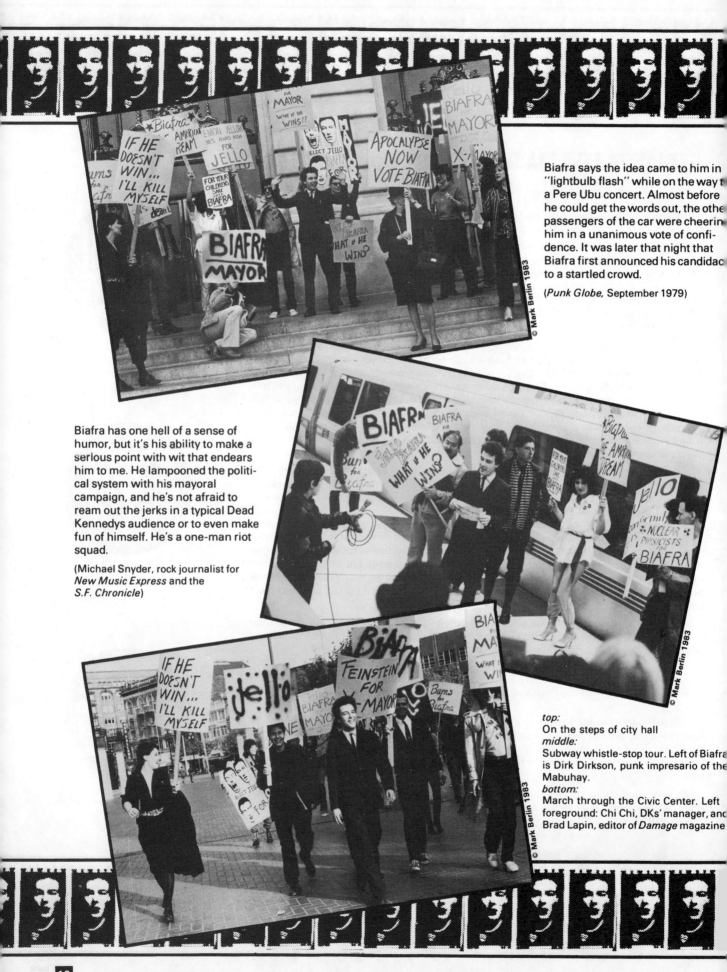

Biafra says the idea came to him in "lightbulb flash" while on the way t a Pere Ubu concert. Almost before he could get the words out, the othe passengers of the car were cheerin him in a unanimous vote of confidence. It was later that night that Biafra first announced his candidac to a startled crowd.

(*Punk Globe,* September 1979)

Biafra has one hell of a sense of humor, but it's his ability to make a serious point with wit that endears him to me. He lampooned the political system with his mayoral campaign, and he's not afraid to ream out the jerks in a typical Dead Kennedys audience or to even make fun of himself. He's a one-man riot squad.

(Michael Snyder, rock journalist for *New Music Express* and the *S.F. Chronicle*)

top:
On the steps of city hall
middle:
Subway whistle-stop tour. Left of Biafra is Dirk Dirkson, punk impresario of the Mabuhay.
bottom:
March through the Civic Center. Left foreground: Chi Chi, DKs' manager, and Brad Lapin, editor of *Damage* magazine

Yes, Johnny Rotten, Joe Strummer, Poly Styrene and that lot may have made a contribution to the socio-political evolution of modern youth, but it took a Yank to actually represent the international pogo party in the election.

(Jack Basher, *NME,* September 1, 1979)

On the campaign trail.
top:
Shaking babies (and kissing hands)
bottom:
"Cleaning up the campaign" (vacuuming in front of Mayor Feinstein's house)

© Target Video 1983

BravEar:
You can't just drop out. People tried doing that in the sixties. They wouldn't have anything to do with it and just dropped out. But if you pull yourself out of the system, it still continues to perpetuate itself and it always catches up with ya. . .
Vic Bondi:
Right, exactly. You can't pull yourself out, you have to change it.

(Interview with Articles of Faith from *BravEar,* a California fanzine, issue #5, winter 1983)

© Mark Berlin 1983

This spaghetti banquet at the Mabuhay raised all the funds for Biafra's campaign.

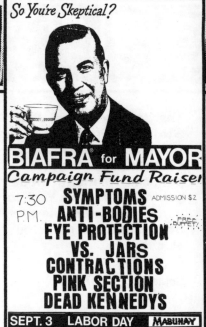
So You're Skeptical?

BIAFRA for **MAYOR**
Campaign Fund Raiser

7:30 P.M. ADMISSION $2

**SYMPTOMS
ANTI-BODIES
EYE PROTECTION
VS. JARS
CONTRACTIONS
PINK SECTION
DEAD KENNEDYS**

FREE BUFFET.

SEPT. 3 LABOR DAY MABUHAY

© Bruce Slesinger 1983

© Mark Berlin 1983

Rock star candidate
and his gorgeous
fiancee!

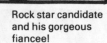

In calling for approval of the bill, Supervisor
Quentin Kopp (his real name) claimed the
practice of using bizarre ballot names is
''another example of what makes people
laugh when they talk about San Francisco.''

(*S.F. Chronicle,* 3/15/83)

(Kopp is yet another example.)

GO TO THE POLLS
and
VOTE
JELLO
"IT IS YOUR DUTY"

© Ephemera 1979

A man who offers nothing and takes nothing
would be an improvement over vested
interest gluttons of established party
politics. . .who promise everything and still
have nothing to offer.

(Viola Weinberg, KZAP/KTIM deejay)

© Target Video 1983

Sleeve art from *Kill The Poor*

© Winston Smith

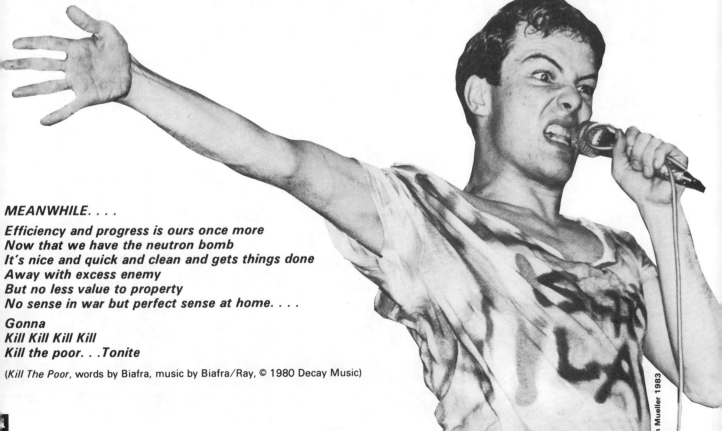

MEANWHILE. . . .

Efficiency and progress is ours once more
Now that we have the neutron bomb
It's nice and quick and clean and gets things done
Away with excess enemy
But no less value to property
No sense in war but perfect sense at home. . . .

Gonna
Kill Kill Kill Kill
Kill the poor. . .Tonite

(*Kill The Poor*, words by Biafra, music by Biafra/Ray, © 1980 Decay Music)

Erich Mueller 1983

Therese backstage at the 1979 Clash concert at Kezar Pavilion, dressed for the occasion....

Meanwhile, Jello, on stage, undressed *by* the occasion.

So you been to school
For a year or two
And you know you've seen it all
In daddy's car
Thinkin' you'll go far
Back East your type don't crawl
Play ethnicky jazz
To parade your snazz
On your five grand stereo
Braggin' that you know
How the niggers feel cold
And the slums got so much soul
It's time to taste what you most fear
Right Guard will not help you here
Brace yourself my dear. . . .
It's a holiday in Cambodia
It's tough, kid, but it's life
It's a holiday in Cambodia
Don't forget to pack a wife

(*Holiday in Cambodia*, words by Biafra,
music by Biafra/Ray/Flouride/Slesinger, © 1980 Decay Music)

Unpublished sleeve for ''Holiday in Cambodia''

© Winston Smith 1983

© f· Stop Fitzgerald 1983

HONEYMOON IN CAMBODIA…?

Shadows were long and a crescent moon was visible in the sky at twilight on this past All Hallows' Eve. And in the Cypress Lawn Cemetery, south of San Francisco, something funny was happening.

It was the marriage of one Jello Biafra, singer and chief ghoul for The Dead Kennedys, to Therese Soder, once teenage leader of the late, unlamented psycho-poppers, The Situations, now full-time Kennedys consort.

The graveyard was overrun with more than 300 living celebrants and around 3000 of the deceased variety. Basic black was *de rigueur* for all, with pink hair and plastic penis-noses among the chic concessions to fashion. The rosy-cheeked bride was decked out in a funereal Victorian taffeta number and her mottled main squeeze sported a nightshade cape and Abe Lincoln stovepipe hat, befitting his political bent. Biafra has not been quick to forget his three per cent share of the popular vote in San Francisco's last mayoral election. Nor have his befuddled but beaming parents.

Mr. and Mrs. B------flew in from Colorado to see their boy and his betrothed united in unholy matrimony, and they were joined by Mr. and Mrs. Soder. Mr. B------, a bearded, amiable fellow, spoke highly of Biafra's innate morality.

"He doesn't drink, smoke or take drugs," said Jello's dad. "Of course, this is a special occasion."

"But this sort of sensationalism is hard on his mother," admitted Jello's mom, a prim, bookish-looking woman.

"It's so exciting," said the bride's mother, adding: "It has as much chance at success as any other marriage these days."

The wedding party mounted the steps of a handy mausoleum surrounded by looming palm trees. Bride and groom blushed with the glow of a few stiff drinks. "Gimme a hit off that beer," barked the demure Therese as she reached the hastily-improvised altar.

"Neither of you is gay, right?" asked Bruce Loose, front-man for California's atonal answer to PiL, Flipper. "No," growled Biafra, "get on with it!" Loose is an ordained minister of the Universal Life Church, a mail-order ministry, so he was tapped to perform the ceremony.

"Before I go any further," said Loose, "does anyone here object to the union of these two lovely young people?" "Yeah!" shouted half of the crowd in unison. "Tough shit," said Loose.

"Do you, Therese, take this screaming faggot as your unlawful wedded hubby, in sickness and in health, especially in sickness, until your mutual karma gets fucked up?" demanded Loose. "Hey! I said I wasn't gay!" yelped Biafra. "Don't get wise, man," Therese warned. "I do."

"Do you, Biafra, take this creature of the night as your wifey, no matter how ugly she looks in the morning when she wakes up?" "I do," he said, with a touch of resignation.

"I had to gouge him into marriage with Mace and bullets," explained Therese after the traditional kissing-of-the-bride and throwing-of-the-rice, followed by the drinking-of-the-tequila. She passed a half-pint flask to Biafra and continued: "We were engaged for over two years, and we plan to have a hell of a time for another five or six years. Perhaps we'll spend the night in some sleazy motel. But first, on to Target to get smashed. Who's got the drugs?"

The reception was held at the headquarters of Target Video, whose production wing was responsible for the DK footage which was projected onto a wall as the guests arrived. Refreshments consisted of a variety of sugar-coated breakfast cereals, straight from the box, including Alpha Bits, Banana Flavored Frosted Flakes, Cocoa Krispies and Froot Loops, washed down with case after case of cheap beer. Entertainment was provided by D.O.A., the blistering, blustering punk band from Vancouver, and a food fight that left the dance floor covered with multi-colored crumbs and our groom smeared with the wedding cake that had read "R.I.P. Therese and Biafra."

"Oh, dear," fretted Jello's mom. "That cape has to go to the cleaners now. You know, I made it for him. I suppose it will end up in the Jello Biafra Archives at the University of Colorado library. For some reason, they've let me accumulate quite a collection of his memorabilia there in a spare corner."

A journalist from one of the Bay Area daily newspapers approached Biafra, as he wiped the icing off his cape. "Well, where's the lucky couple going from here? Holiday in Cambodia?"

"No," spat Biafra, glaring at the reporter and leaving the building with his new wife in tow. "Honeymoon in Libya."

—MICHAEL SNYDER

(*The New Musical Express*, 28th November, 1981)

CUTTER LABORATORIES
and
DANCING SQUID GENETIC
RESEARCH CENTER
proudly announce the marriage of
their offspring:

THERESE SODER
and
JELLO BIAFRA

united in unholy matrimony

Saturday October 31,
the year of no lord, 1981

Motorcade departs from the corner
of Army St. and Valencia for the cere-
monial grounds no later than 4:15 PM.
Please bring transportation if possible.

Reception will be held afterwards

Please bring this invitation with you

[artist unknown]

Parents of the bride, bride, groom, and parents of the groom.

26

The wedding cake by (center) Stannous Flouride fueled the food fight (right).

IDOL (DEAD KENNEDYS VERSION)   ©1979 & ©1981 WINSTON SMITH

WHEN PLAYED BACKWARDS, DEAD KENNEDYS RECORDS CONTAIN PARTS OF THE LORD'S PRAYER*

*THANKS TO DAVE SHERIDAN

Roman Szolkowski

TROUSER PRESS/March 1983   7

© Jerry Gardner 1983

IF YOU LOVE GOD BURN A CHURCH

© Winston Smith 1983

29

Sleeve art for Plastic Surgery Disasters (and far right)

CONFLAGRATION OF PHILOSOPHY

As Biafra told Ira Kaplan (*New York Rocker*, July/Aug. 1981), "Anybody who doesn't use art as a weapon is not an artist." This, perhaps, was the original key to DK dominance: *consistent* use of the stage as a launching pad for political missiles. From the first they billed themselves as an "antistupidity" band, taking every opportunity in print and on the air as well as onstage to expound what has come to be known as the Vacant Stranger Theory:

People who are more interested in building cocoons for themselves than in trying to get rid of the problems they're building cocoons to keep out...are the ones most openly proud of being stupid..."I will one day fall in love. I will one day have a job that I like"...They'll either just quietly try to ride it out until they crack up or they'll turn into a John Hinckley...We glorify the vacant stranger as one outlet to mental freedom.

(*N.Y. Rocker*, ibid.)

The real criminals, see, aren't the Vacant Strangers, but the mindless authoritarians who run things by default. A note of nostalgic lamentation even creeps in at times:

> Americans as a whole have no soul. . .There's a certain pride in being from a certain stock and a certain region, and even in being able to do things in a certain way and do them well, that we don't have in this country.
> (Biafra interviewed by Peter Belsito, *Ego* #2, July 1982)

> You just have to look at the difference between people like Eisenhower and Haig; Eisenhower was genuinely elected President, and his last statement to the public was, "Beware of the military-industrial complex." Haig will ask people to embrace it.
> (Klaus interviewed in *New Musical Express*, 10/17/81)

Are you handcuffed to your secretary?

Sound familiar? Actually these sentiments make sense: American liberalism applied to the historical conditions of the 60s had a radical charge, whereas against the background of the 80s it adopts an almost conservative coloration. You know: the Individual, government by and for the People, self-determination, freedom of expression and from religious encroachment, equal opportunity. . .If you're *cool*, like Scott Bolgiano in *1981* #6 (May 1-14, 1981), you laugh at the DKs' "stream of political rhetoric, philosophical claptrap and just plain taunts." Even cooler cats like Tom Carson skip the politics altogether and complain that "what the Dead Kennedys have never assimilated about punk is its melodic beauty" (that has to be the strangest complaint I've ever heard out of a punk writer—from the *Boston Phoenix*, 2/9/82). But it's not as if we've got all those neat old virtues like Freedom in the *bag* or anything; on the contrary, some hideous dark shape is huddled in there and we're afraid to look. . .

The DKs' work, the job of consciousness, is never done. As Mark Leach puts it, Biafra "is genuinely interested in raising the political consciousness of these kids. He could be busy for a long time" (*Shades*, op. cit.). Principles, principles. How can you get ahead with them? How can you look at yourself in the mirror without them?

Much is known about Biafra's origins and opinions and rather less about the origins and opinions of the other band members. When any four guys get together as performers, one is bound to seem more "with it," so to speak, than the rest. The press prefers his company, calls him "articulate," purveys his mug; and gradually he becomes the perceived leader of the group. In the Beatles this role fell to John, in the Pistols to Johnny. Those two were the Thinkers, bursting with *bons mots* and instant philosophies to add luster to whatever they were up to at the moment. If the other three DKs don't agree with Jello's pronouncements, however, they at least seem content to let him represent the band in public.

But there may be a slight hint of sarcasm to be found in an interview with Klaus done in November 1981 by a Roman magazine, *Il Mucchio Selvaggio* (which could mean "The Savage Heap" but is probably intended to be "The Wild Bunch"). The interviewer asks if Jello is always so tirelessly provocative as during their wild gig at the Much More in Rome, and Klaus answers (in Italian!), *"Si, si cerca di instaurare un contatto fra noi ed il pubblico,"* by which he means to say, of course, "Yeah, he tries to establish contact between us and the audience. . ."

By the end of 1980 their first album had been released on the Cherry Red label, a British indie (see Discography). "Fresh Fruit for Rotting Vegetables" sold tens of thousands of copies before finally being released in the U.S. by IRS (International Records Syndicate), with Faulty Products in L.A. as the distributor. Demand for DKs records and appearances grew steadily in power despite the band's grand stands against high ticket prices, restriction of minors from clubs, and the general massification of punk into "New Wave." Without such resistance, Biafra felt the whole business would turn into a job "you have to do if you're going to play for Bill Graham on a seven-foot stage for ten bucks a ticket and watch his goon squad beat up fans for dancing" (*Shades*, op. cit.).

Another reason to shun seven-foot stages is that back flips into the teeth of the audience are more comfortable from a lesser height. There are thousands of punk bands but not many have a lead singer willing to bellydive into the war zone, get stripped to the skin or a pair of ripped briefs, then be passed back across a canopy of hands to the stage, all without missing a lyric. In defense of the other punk bands, though, it must be said that it wasn't long before Biafra tired of this routine. Anything the audience comes to expect— e.g., that Wayne Newton is going to sing "Red Roses for a Blue Lady," that Sam and Dave are going to sing "Soul Man"—gets to be a drag for any performer above the rank of hack. "These jocks had started showing up at the Mab for the sole purpose of stripping me," Biafra laughs. "Clothes are expensive. So now I wear boots instead of shoes, and I wear stronger clothing. We don't want to get like other bands, who tend to withdraw rather dramatically from their crowds."

Not only that, but Biafra and the band are getting older. Yeah, it happens, that's the deal: if you want to live you have to get *older*, if you want to stay young you can drop dead right now.

You'd be surprised how many people think we're serious . . . [Kill The Poor] was number 4 on the charts in Portugal. We think the government promoted it.

—Ray

FIND OUT WHO'S RESPONSIBLE FOR THIS TRASH AND BRING ME THEIR HEADS ON A STICK.

NATIONAL AFFAIRS

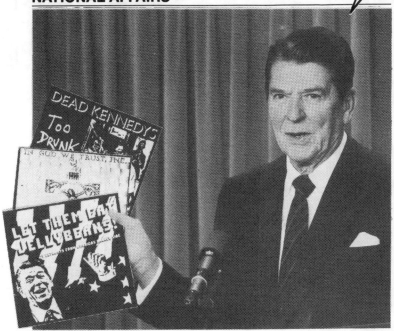

A PRESIDENTIAL ENDORSEMENT
©1983 Winston Smith

"I kind of live for the psychodrama"

© Lynda Burdick 1983

© Bobby Castro 1983

© Karen Filter 1983

"*Anyone can rob a bank.
Anyone can paint a picture.*"

© Craig Dietz 1983

© Ed Colver 1983

© Karen Filter 1983

So here we are, Society extinguishing itself to the strains of ear-shattering, three-chord rock. We had all come for entertainment, but everyone has his own idea of fun. Some people only show up to see how far the other half has gone...

("God, Freud, and PiL," *Watts Up*, UC Berkeley, 12/82, by the aptly named Darwin Davis)

YOUTH: WASTED ON THE YOUNG

Although you can't help but hear echoes of the Pistols' "Holidays in the Sun" in the DKs' "Holiday in Cambodia," the radicalism of American bands is basically a different animal. For one thing, in the British Isles *everyone's* a Marxist—they don't even bother to capitalize it, "marxist" this, "marxist" that. For another thing (hopefully Julie Burchill and Tony Parsons won't throw a tantrum when I say this), Britain's never *had* a revolution, and we *have*. They've got the oldest continuously-ruling monarchy in the world! So how revolutionary can Brits be, really? Bands like Gang of Four and the Clash are great literary revolutionists, with a fine musical vocabulary of revolt as well as an impressive verbal range of negation. Somehow they've got it all down a bit too pat, though—cooked instead of raw. "Irony," blue plate special on the menu of despair. . .

As for the Clash, Tom Carson had it right when he said Combat Rock should now be called Combat Fatigue: "the Clash's romanticism isn't tenable any more, not least because it's running out of real-life objects it can project itself on" (*Village Voice*, 6/15/82).

Yet as Carola Dibbell asks, "What exactly is a leftist rock and roll band supposed to do at this crisis of Western democracy? What can it sell? Information? Sedition? Guilt? Courage? Fear?" (*Village Voice*, 7/27/82)

Well, what do the DKs sell? Tension, probably. And contradictions: alienation/commitment, skepticism/faith, violence/tolerance. Look at their image, out of which Biafra has been plucked and added to the culture's iconography as a half-naked figure plunging like Christ, Fisher of Men, into a sea of body-pistons. Their whole public self projects the tension between Rock's antifascist *message* ("Nazi Punks Fuck Off") and its semifascist *reality* (which "Pink Floyd The Wall" explicitly enacts). "California Uber Alles" probably works the same juices that "Deutschland Ueber Alles" did during its day in the sun not long ago. Biafra hectors the crowd with their ignorance of history, exhorting them to resist racist fascism and fascist racism; meanwhile he dictates absolutely from the stage, secure like all dictators in his ability to arouse our atavisms and possess us through them.

Possession of others is an art of sorts. Charisma you either have or you don't. Biafra has got quantities of it. But it's a tricky thing to maintain. For one thing the mob is always mutating into more resistant strains of Fun-Love. Each time it takes them a little longer to soften up and get, you know, *receptive*. The sound man squeezes his levers hard; small lights squirt and bob across the console. The hall slowly accumulates the necessary density for metamorphosis to occur. Soon the band will start to sweat what looks like blood in the scarlet spotlights. Till then you hang out in the bathroom with its steamy mirrors, a bunch of drunken punkettes letting what's left of their hair down. Where are they getting these clothes? Do they live at home—looking like *that*? Can they hold jobs? I can hear the dinnertable conversation now. . .

. . .Dad wants to know if Rick's going to be home for dinner and Mom says she left the money for his haircut on the kitchen table, so he's probably down at Great Expectations getting the usual $16.95 cut, style and blow-dry. May as well start without him. The hamburgers might dry out if they wait much longer.

It happens right about here. Happens every day, in fact, all over Southern California. Young Rick or Brent or Jeffrey or Mark or Randy or David or Shaun comes in the front door, a little hesitantly, maybe, at first, but once he gets inside......well, what the hell. Too late now anyway. He goes ahead and plunks himself down at the dinner table and waits for the folks to recover the ability to speak after the shock of seeing his head shaved smooth as a spud.

Usually takes a good thirty or forty seconds before they even say anything....have to get their wind back first....unless there'll like maybe be a sister who jumps up from the table and locks herself in her room to cry for about two hours and scream about how none of her

© Craig Dietz 1983

The pure products of America go crazy.

—William Carlos Williams

friends are ever going to talk to her again....which sort of gets the ice broken. (Nobody knows for sure why it is, but mohawks are good for about a minute and a half of glassed-over eyes and erratic breathing. Something about the first glimpse of Junior with that centerstripe bristling up out of a field of stubble really coldcocks 'em.)

...Parents of the mohawk kids more often than not remembered Travis Bickle from *Taxi Driver*—it's funny how many people have seen that movie. But that first involuntary jerk to the imagebank lodged right near the top of the spine, the joker that jumped forth from the deck, skullfaced and somber, that staring, accusing face from the past—that was something nearly all of them shared.

(excerpted from "Beachpunks & Skinheads: A Howl of Victory" by Bart Bull, *New Times,* Phoenix, Ariz., May 13-19, 1981)

Hang around long enough, of course, and you see plenty of graduations from the Scene *per se.* But despite the fantastic turnover rate and even more fantastic rate of influx, some kids—not actually kids but "cases"—remain behind, beached surf punks who've ridden their last wave, it seems. They come out night after night; they hold sullen court in the girls' room, half-heartedly pushing smack or what passes for it to girls who just want to piss and get it over with.

The DKs' drug of choice is adrenalin: "what you get when you're destroying private property. It's what you get when you throw bottles at somebody's new white Cadillac" (Biafra, interviewed in *1981,* op. cit.). They consider the growing use of harder and harder drugs available on the streets to be a government plot. "One of the main reasons the DKs have been around for so long is none of the members have ever had a drug problem," Biafra told Peter Belsito (*Ego* #2, op. cit.). Talking to *Fallout* shortly after Reagan's election in 1980, he went so far as to say, "Mark my words. If any member of the Dead Kennedys is found dead of a drug overdose or a car crash—a government agency is behind it."

Here I am reminded of the legendary Michael Kowalsky, founder of the band UXA (United Experiments of America). Perhaps being political in the U.S. means choosing which conspiracy to believe in. Here we hear Michael give Jello a run for his money in the political department, piecing oddments of info into a paranoid afghan:

> Don't you think punk rock is one of the first trends in America that isn't directly manipulated by the government? After all, they *did* give LSD away. 1964 was when the CIA experimented at Stanford with LSD, and 1964 was when it exploded on the streets.
> (Interview in *Search & Destroy* #6, March 1978)

If the recipe for legends is *Die young,* Kowalsky was a master chef. "After Michael Kowalsky's death," Biafra regretfully recalls, "the intense camaraderie of the Scene really unraveled."

I hate to put it this way, but by their political and anti-drug stance the Dead Kennedys seem to be saying they *care.* Aw, gee—that's pretty uncool. On the other hand, you're lucky anybody cares about you, punk. If you don't care, sho'nuf nobody else gone to. Cause we know, don't we, that you're hoping Punk will make your mom go grey (if you only knew where Mom *was* tonight!) To punk out is to tattoo I AM A FAILURE all over your rotten selfish parents. The grieving members of the L.A.-based support group "Parents of Punkers" know the bitter truth of this only too well, as they come together in their mutual pain to explain away their sins of omission. *Why me, oh Lord?...*

> The most primitive anxieties concerning the sacred distinction between nature and culture can be summoned up by the emergence of such a group [as punks].
> (Dick Hebdige, *Subculture: The Meaning of Style,* 1979)

At least you very much hope so. The problem is, are your parents capable of distinguishing between "nature" and "culture" any more? As a member of the band Fifth Column told a friend of mine, "Whaddya think *you'd* be like if you were brought up by a ten-year-old?"

*Mark my words. If any member of the Dead Kennedys
is found dead of a drug overdose or a car crash—a
government agency is behind it.*

—Biafra

© Laura Levine 1983

FOLLOW THE EXPERTS

"Trust Your Mechanic"

WE GOT A DRUG
WE'RE GONNA TRY IT OUT ON YOU
WON'T MAKE YOU DIE
IT'LL GETCHA JUST A LITTLE BIT SICK

GOT A HEAD COLD
GOT A CHEST COLD
AND IT'S THREE DAYS OLD
GOIN' ON FOREVER
MAKE YOU HAZY
MAKE YOU CRAZY
FOR DAYS AND DAYS AND DAYS AND
   DAYS AND DAYS
AND YEARS

(*Government Flu,* words and music by Biafra,
© 1982 Decay Music)

© f-Stop Fitzgerald 1983

You had people just sitting down waiting to have a good time, and we were not going to allow that. We went out and knocked all these tables over and showered them with beer and shampooed them with their cigarettes.

(Biafra, *NY Rocker*, July/August 1981)

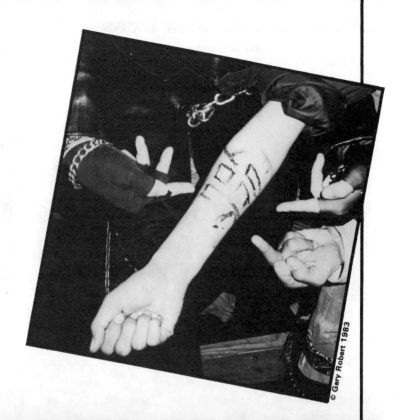

© Gary Robert 1983

*We know you're hoping
Punk will make your
mom go grey. . .*

© Ed Colver 1983

Skinheads lose their laces

BRIGHTON, England — Scores of young "skinheads" had to shuffle through the streets of this seaside resort because police confiscated their bootlaces to keep them from rioting. Police yesterday swooped down on trains, automobiles, motorcycles and scooters carrying youths, _____ for a spring holiday and forced them to surre_____ camp_____ repetition _____

Klaus, D.H., Ray, Jello *Foto Guglielmi*

S.F. Sunday Examiner & Chronicle ngra-
Datebook, Sunday, June 28, 1981

sa, come potrebbe essere lo stesso?».

«Ed il modo di vestirsi, la «punk-fashion?».

«Non è come in Inghilterra, in California i kids preferiscono una maglietta ai giubbotti ne la "beach-punk" fashion».

«L'attuale situazione mu californiana, la new-wave, bra diversa dall'inizio?».

«Adesso in America, ed ticolare in California, molte più punk-bands di non vengono soltanto g borghi delle solite gra ma da tutto il paese, d nere di posti.

Ho preparato un a ative Tentacl

bile?».

«Sì, si cerca di instaurare un contatto vero fra noi ed il pubblico. C'è una cosa che vorrei dire: il prezzo del biglietto in questo concerto era troppo alto. Di solito cerchiamo di fare in '- che non superi le 5000 lire, — ci siamo riusci- ruesto è

il parziale fallimento dello show romano ci sarebbe da discutere a lungo, ma forse è inutile farlo, cer tamente, comunque, sarebbe stato illogico pretendere che un gruppo oltraggioso e violento come i Dead Kennedys non scatenasse le reazioni di qualche esaltato, ma Much More si è veramente toc- '- Forse è propno dy morti», che aglie tem-

andando ieri al "Tube", (u le romano - n.d.r.) abbiam dei complessi, e ne a scelto uno che ci piace farlo suonare prima di n

«Qualche nome di band cane che ritieni interessa

«Feederz, da Phoeni na. Minor Threat e S Washington D.C., e poi niani: Flipper, Black Fl Anche i D.O.A. ottimi, ond

'Word of mouth' gives Cherry Red unlikely hit

THE BBC has banned it, so has the Independent Broadcasting Authority. *Sounds*, *NME* and a leading fanzine refused to take advertisements mentioning its title. And a number of leading record chains refused to stock it. But despite these problems, the Dead Kennedy's single, Too Drunk To Fuck, has made it into the charts and sales at press time had passed the 20,000 mark.

"Basically, it's all been achieved through word of mouth." Cherry Red's Iain McNay told *MW*. "We did not want to compromise with ads in the consumer papers that didn't spell out the title. The band felt that that would be the kind of control they would get from a major record company.

"But we felt it was vir...

also the first record of ours to through Pinnacle which has be working extra hard on it "

The Dead Kennedys album, Fre Fruit For Rotting Vegetables (BRE 10), also on Cherry Red, is sti doing well in Japan, Australia an New Zealand. And in the UK sale are past the 70,000 mark while in Finland the album is in the Top 10.

The controversial single is to be released in eight territories and McNa him Sweden has told airp extensive

B

DREXEL TR
November

LIVELY ARTS

JIM MORRISON

MARK NAFTALIN

WOLFMAN JACK

By Joel Selvin

OUR BAD boy punks, the **Dead Kennedys**, keep raising a fuss over in not-so-jolly England, a country that used to pride itself on tolerating eccentricity, as long as it was kept out of the streets, where it could scare the horses.

Not only has the BBC banned the Kennedys' Top 30 British hit, "Too Drunk To F--k," but the announcers can't even bring themselves to utter the group's vile name, instead opting for the disclaimer, "a band calling themselves the Dead Kennedys." In Bristol, police raided a record store carrying T-shirts bearing the record's title, which were confiscated. In Manchester, another record store was busted just for displaying the offensive album cover in the store window and local officials ar considering pressing obscenity charges.

SOUNDS

DEAD KENNEDYS: the San Francisco cult band who have been widely featured in *Sounds* playlists for ages now, are to have their 'California Uber Alies' 45 licensed to Fast Products in two weeks time. The first pressing of the record has now completely sold out. Meanwhile the band's singer, Biafra, is intending to stand for Mayor in San Francisco. His intention is said to be 'dead serious'. How could we think otherwise?

California Uber Alles / With The Dogs, Dead Kenne (Decay Music); This Franciso band has been gett alot of attention in reports fro the West Coast for about a yea now. We are beginning to hea about them locally becaus themainstream press likes to sensationalize their name, Dead Kennedys, without thinking about its significance. Typical. The English have made this single a top-seller on the underground charts, which is a good reference as to its quality. An even better one: While in the Mid-West 'ly, the Clash were in the T.V. show 'ked if there "punk"

TO YURP

Yurp—yep, we still care a lot how we're thought of over there. Going to England, for a rock band, is like faring to Benares for a pious Hindu. And even though Continental Yurpeens have never been much good at rock 'n' roll themselves, their opinion has such *cachet* it's highly valued. The Kennedys went to Yurp at least three times between 1980 and 1982. In Britain their name alone—"a very nice little thorn in our side," as Biafra proudly calls it—got them banned from 180 venues in a single week, and Eastern Yurpeen authorities won't hear of them penetrating the Iron Curtain, but in the Low Countries, Germany, France, Italy, Austria, Sweden, and Finland, the response has been good. In Finland especially—which is odd because the Finns are famed for their melancholy and their habit of drinking themselves into a shitfaced gloom by 2 or 3 in the winter-sunlit morning.

Last year in Berlin the DKs caused consternation to some and wicked delight to others by hiring an all-Turkish crew and playing Turkish-owned halls. (The Turks are the niggers of West Germany.) In Italy they inspired such violent mob scenes that the aforementioned mag *Il Mucchio Selvaggio,* while acknowledging "l'incredibile presenza scenica di Jello," was moved to cluck, "*Forse è proprio vero, cari 'Kennedy morti,' che 'chi semina vento raccoglie tempesta'*" (For it is quite true, dear "Dead Kennedys," that "he who sows the wind reaps the whirlwind"). Song titles may mean different things to different cultures, too. About "Kill the Poor," Ray remarked, "You'd be surprised how many people think we're serious. That song was number 4 on the charts in Portugal. We think the government promoted it" (*Boston Phoenix,* op. cit.).

Their biggest impression has been made on the U.K. London's Cherry Red was the first label to sign the Dead Kennedys. According to *Sounds* (9/81), one British fan was "bound over to keep the peace for one year" by magistrates after he was discovered wearing a "Too Drunk to Fuck" t-shirt. Shops carrying such t-shirts or the record itself were raided, all posters advertising the single were torn down, even *Sounds* and *NME* refused to carry ads for it. Airplay was nonexistent, yet "Too Drunk to Fuck" mounted the British charts with handsome vigor in late '81—most likely because it deals with drinking, which you can tell is the fave rave of British pastimes if you've ever joined a gang of Brits pub-crawling. No, but seriously, there's nothing like a band banned to light a fire under a record. A bullet is waiting. . .

In any event, it's fair to say that the DKs have a goodly number of fans in England. Julie Burchill is not among them, we dare say. We can almost hear her fulminating now: "This snotnosed vapid babbling rabble of American hippies with their vulgar mass palate and their moronic driveling nonsense about 'freedom' (to do what??) and 'stupidity' (their own, surely!)," etc., etc., or words to that effect. Actually the one quotable line I could exhume from *The Face* concerning the DKs was a supercilious comment about Biafra being "a polite and cooperative American," and I don't know why I'm even quoting that one.

What has happened to many American bands and artists also happened to the Dead Kennedys: while Biafra's mayoral campaign may have given them name recognition in select parlors of America, it was the cross-fertility of their successes in Yurp which made them musically credible. *Incredibile, ma vero.*

*We'd never think of imitating a band that **imitates**—that's all English bands do to be in rock'n'roll, is imitate American culture. They don't **know** American culture and then they accuse us of imitating!*

(Exene of X, quoted in *Search & Destroy* #10, 1979)

What's it like to be an American?

—Jah Wobble

© Sue Brisk 1983

© f-Stop Fitzgerald 1983

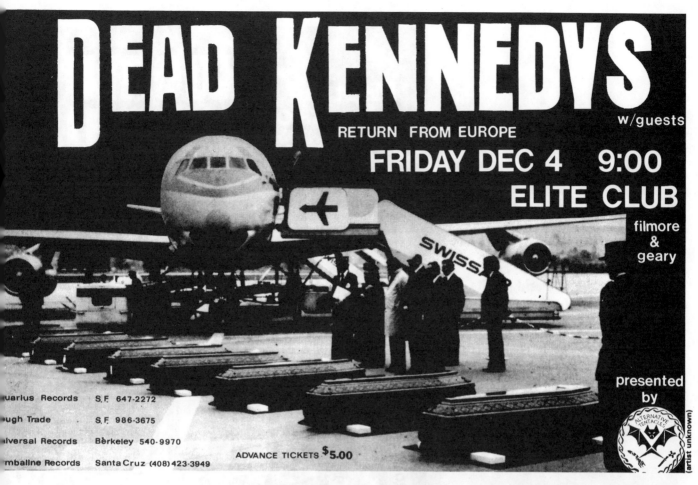

DEAD KENNEDYS

w/guests

RETURN FROM EUROPE

FRIDAY DEC 4   9:00
ELITE CLUB

filmore
&
geary

SWISS

presented
by

ALTERNATIVE TENTACLES

(artist unknown)

uarius Records   S.F. 647-2272

ugh Trade   S.F. 986-3675

iversal Records   Berkeley 540-9970

mbaline Records   Santa Cruz (408) 423-3949

ADVANCE TICKETS $5.00

*American culture—
what's that?*

*I didn't think there
was an American
culture.*

(PiL, interviewed by "the
press," San Francisco,
September 1982)

© Lynda Burdick 1983

© Ann Summa 1983

In the name of world peace
In the name of world profits
America pumps up our
secret police
America wants fuel
To get it, it needs puppets
So what's ten million dead?
If it's keeping out the Russians

(*Bleed For Me*, words and music by Biafra,
Ray, Flouride, Peligro, ©1982 Decay Music)

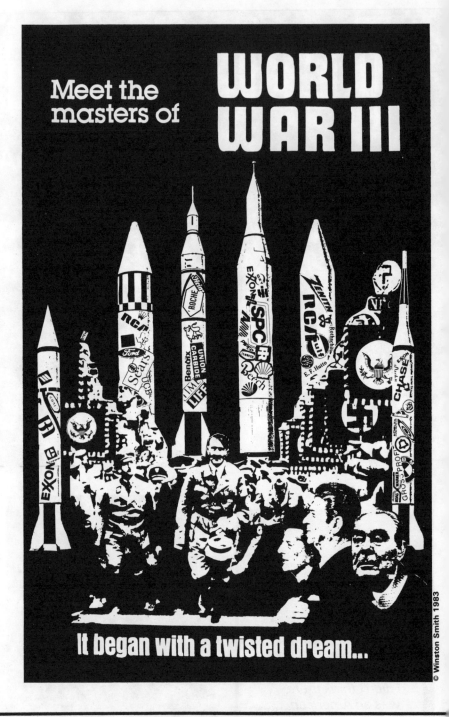

It began with a twisted dream...

© Winston Smith 1983

Where everything is bad, it must be good to know the worst.

—motto of Club Foot

IF YOU LOVE YOUR CAR DIE FOR IT.

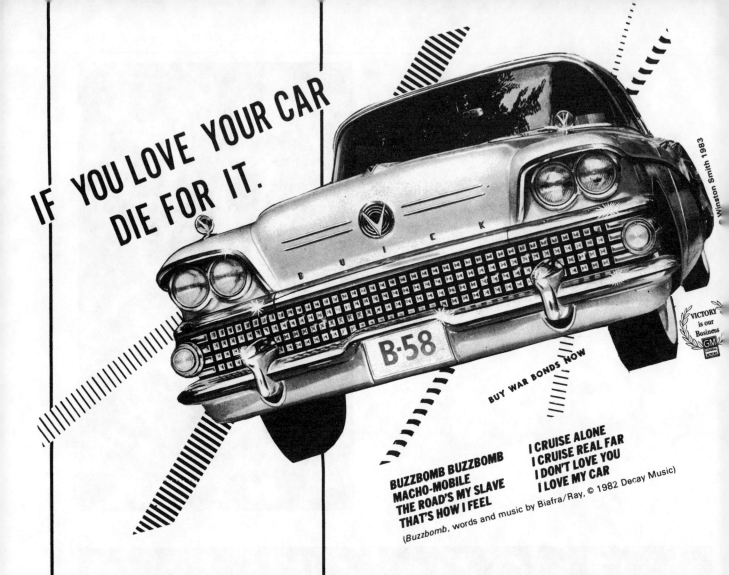

© Winston Smith 1983

B·58

VICTORY is our Business
GM GENERAL MOTORS

BUY WAR BONDS NOW

BUZZBOMB BUZZBOMB
MACHO-MOBILE
THE ROAD'S MY SLAVE
THAT'S HOW I FEEL

I CRUISE ALONE
I CRUISE REAL FAR
I DON'T LOVE YOU
I LOVE MY CAR

(Buzzbomb, words and music by Biafra/Ray, © 1982 Decay Music)

MICHAEL HENNESSEY, sheriff, San Francisco:

I love the car I currently own. It's a 1970 VW convertible painted Hershey bar brown. I bought it on D-Day in 1970 and I've driven it 120,000 miles. I've driven it back and forth from here to my home town in Iowa a half a dozen times; I've built it and rebuilt it. I love that car. It's a beautiful car. It is the greatest car for driving around the city on one of those rare warm nights with the top down and the stereo blasting out Mahler or the Dead Kennedys.

(*S.F. Examiner*, November 21, 1982)

Dog bite
On my leg
Not right
Supposed to beg

(*Dog Bite*, words and music by
Flouride, © 1981 Decay Music)

© Jerry Gardner 1983

© Erich Mueller 1983

The San Francisco Club of the Deaf was one of those fun places that fold and leave you wondering ever afterwards if it was really the perfect venue, or if you just used to have a better class of friends. The live album recorded there during 1979, "Can You Hear Me?," bears the same relation to the gigs held at that club as a lingering smell of stale Gitanes bears to a night with your French lover. Yet it was on this "showcase" that the Dead Kennedys made their recording debut with early versions of "Police Truck" and "Straight As" that sound as if they were taped inside a moving cement mixer. Not that they sound any worse than the other five bands on the album.

When you hear it live and blasting through the usual low-grade sound system, even catchy "California Uber Alles" is difficult to distinguish. After some judicious *mixage* in the studio, though, a song like that stands out with a memorability reminiscent of the Pistols' "Anarchy in the U.K." or "Problems." Even the Brits liked that tune. They called it "Wagnerian punk" with a "glorious, Pistolean riff that is fat and beefy" (like English cuisine). Pistolean! Talk about your ultimate accolade. A *Sounds* critic (8/11/79) confessed, "This is the best yankee punk single I've *ever* heard. It's funny, it's hard, it's loud, it's imaginative without being contrived, it's as dirty as a bear's bum in production. . ."

Overall production quality owes most to Ray's skill, but certain recent cuts have been engineered by L.A.'s Geza X (notable for transforming what must have been a traumatic toilet-training into artistry on "Mean Mr. Mommy Man"). Many of the more obscure musical influences found in their work probably got there via Klaus, who knows just about all there is to know about obscure music. Biafra writes all the lyrics and usually comes up with something hummable, and he does have that voice to unleash like an attack dog. "Fresh Fruit for Rotting Vegetables" confirmed what audiences can (almost) hear

live: the DKs put together a great rock 'n' roll song. They're individualized, well-crafted, lined with tight memorable riffs, and sung in a decent roaring tenor that sounds, not a baleful 14 years old, but mature with satire and sort of *authoritative,* you know? You can always tell a DKs song; how many bands are that distinctive? You can always tell Biafra's voice; his sneers and snarls are nuanced, his ironies seldom as leaden and obvious as punk taste generally runs.

Following "Fresh Fruit" came a number of singles, including "Holiday in Cambodia"/"Police Truck," "Bleed for Me"/"Life Sentence," and "Too Drunk to Fuck"/"The Prey." In early 1982 Faulty Products issued a press release for a new 8-song EP called "In God We Trust, Inc.," which read in part: "Once again, they've come up with a record that puts rock-n-roll in the same catagory as blasphemy and twisted sex crimes." *Sic.* This type of hype could be what Biafra was referring to when he told Peter Belsito: "Considering their goals and the way they approach them, I'm still very puzzled as to why [Faulty Products is] interested in us at all. I mean they know full well we're *violently* anti-corporation." "In God We Trust" was nominally on the DKs' own Alternative Tentacles label, which Biafra calls "a rinkydink attempt at a record label—never rely on a musician to come through with anything," so it looks as if they'll have to suffer their corporate bedfellows a little while longer.

The "God" record *looks* regular—an EP isn't an LP, of course—but still, the player arm has scarcely settled before the grooves have angrily flung it off again. One critic pointed out that the length of all eight songs comes to less than that of "Inna Gadda da Vida." Many reviewers accounted for the incredible speed with which the sides of this disc fly by on grounds of *urgency*: the Republic is in mortal danger from Reaganites and Moral Majoritarians, there's no time to lose. And the consensus among DK admirers

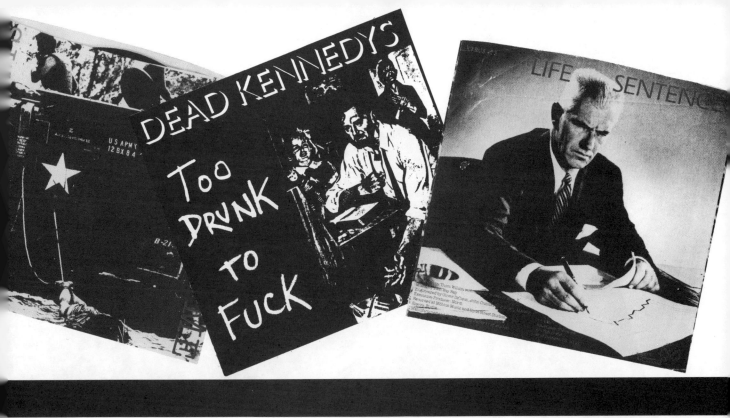

was that this EP was "the closest thing we've had to a 'protest' album since the mid-60s." But lots of reviewers disliked the record. One called it "a cigarette burn in the carpet of American art." The best pan was Stu Hackel's in *The Ticket*: "I suppose they're not trying to be important. If anything, their message is not that they are committed but perhaps that they should be." Very subtle, Stu! It's good to see that punk is keeping at least the art of invective alive.

Speaking of invective and the like, the Dead Kennedys of course are considered *truly* dead—finished—kaput in many avant-garde circles. They're supportive to a fault of other bands, constantly quoting them and pushing their music and extolling their virtues. Where would Flipper be without the attention lavished on them by the DKs? Jello once told somebody that "one of the ways to avoid being resented in San Francisco is to continue to pop up at some of the real, real underground places to play" (*N.Y. Rocker*, op. cit.), but even that doesn't work. The DKs are uncool, political, committed. Whereas "post"-punk, whatever else it may be, is sheer flat pop *acceptance* of the rules of the game. As for those particular snot pups capable of wearing a button like "Blondie is the name of the *band*"—hell, the Dead Kennedys never existed for them anyway. In a scene where you're supposed to treat only the very latest hardcore tape played on the local punk station as *the* music which supposedly blasts everything everyone else has ever done clear out of the pool and into oblivion—well, it's kinda tough to *hang in there*, you know? A thankless task, really. Disgruntled fans crown you with beer bottles, disgruntled "new" bands denounce you musically. One local up-and-coming bunch of young contenders has a song out called "I Hate the Dead Kennedys." Well, of *course* they hate them! We all do. We only really like dead people. Living celebrities oppress us; dead ones make us feel good and cause us pleasant chills of nostalgia.

By dying, people prove they know how to do the right thing. As expressed by Miss Amy Linden in Boston's *Take It!*,

> It's the old punk rationale of we love you when you can't play & no one sees you & you're starving but now that you're good & you're reaching thousands you suck fuck you sell out sell out sell out.

It's not that the DKs aren't criticizable—oh no. Even we their biographers—or anyway I—have bones to pick with them ideologically and so forth. Their targets are too easy, all over the map, and sometimes mutually contradictory. For example, how can you desire to deindustrialize the nation and at the same time feel sentimental about poor people? How can you bitch about Pol Pot and the Khmer Rouge and at the same time oppose U.S. efforts to contain Communism in Southeast Asia? If you want to see what a country really looks like when it's taken over by its left-wing petty-bourgeois intelligentsia, do take that holiday in Cambodia.

Another basic bone of contention found repeatedly in Biafra's raps is the idea that *creativity is crushed out of kids by the system*. Not exactly: instead, the System from parents on down systematically evades its responsibilities by throwing kids back on their own hypothetical "creativity" almost as a last resort, substituting "self-expression" for mental discipline and impressionistic "feelings" for hard knowledge. Express myself? When I'm 9 years old? Express *what*? I'd be a lot better off learning math and grammar. Where do the DKs think the innumerable labile legions who call themselves Artists are coming from? At any rate, a basic staple of Biafra's rap is "My favorite people are the ones who are willing to tell us they think we're making a mistake rather than saying, 'I agree with everything you say'" (*Ego*, op. cit.). I just thought I'd take him up on that.

© Richard McCaffrey 1983

Clothes are expensive. So now I wear boots instead of shoes, and I wear stronger clothing. We don't want to get like other bands, who tend to withdraw rather dramatically from their crowds.

—Biafra

© Ed Colver 1983

© Ed Colver 1983

The crowded future stings my eyes
I still find time to exercise
In uniform with two white stripes

Unlock my section of the sand
It's fenced off to the water's edge
I clamp a gasmask on my head

On my beach at night
Bathe in my moonlight

I squash dead fish between my toes
Try not to step on any bones
I turn around and I go home

I slip back through my basement door
Switch off all that I own below
Dive in my scalding wooden tub

My own beach at night
Electric moonlight

There will always be a moon
Over Marin

(*Moon Over Marin*, words and music by Biafra, Ray,
© 1982 Decay Music)

© Sammy Zebra 1983

55

© Erich Mueller 1983

© Ed Colver 1983

What's wrong with this picture?

© Winston Smith 1983

Consider the name of lead singer Jello Biafra. Can you think of a sharper description of U.S.-Third World relations?

(Doug Simmons in *Boston Phoenix*, April 21, 1981)

© f-Stop Fitzgerald 1983

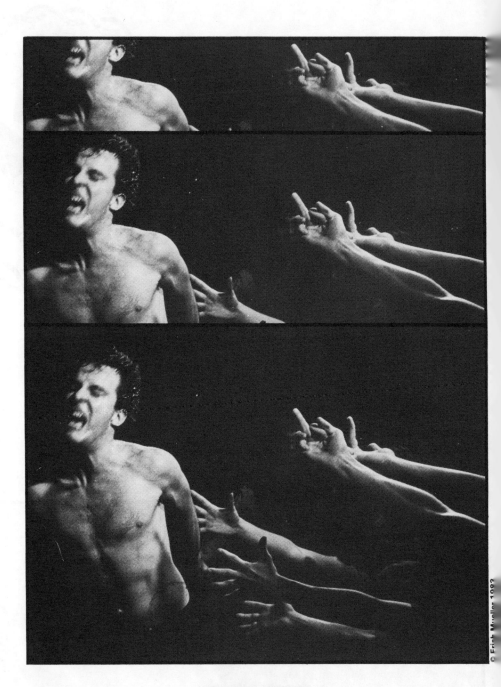

RECENTLY

"The shirtless and sweaty Biafra, looking like a putty-muscled demon. . ." wrote Doug Simmons in *The Boston Phoenix*, "had two attendants whose sole chore was to drag him, often by the ankles, back onstage. . ." *Noblesse oblige*: let anyone else try to get too demonic at a DKs gig and the band is all over them like flies on catshit. Let a guy wearing a swastika or shooting Nazi salutes get too close to the stage and Biafra might grab him by the kerchief round his neck and haul him up for ridicule—"Idiot! Who do you think's gonna be the first to go when fascism comes to power?" Let a serious bloody fight erupt and the band'll stop playing and shout at the battling titans that if they want a real fight why don't they go beat up a bank president, for chrissake? The DKs have no truck with bad punk politics; they demand most audibly that Nazi punks fuck off. And they deeply believe that slam-dancing, like its cousin S&M, calls for the proper sportsmanship rules and limits to be observed. Remember kids, you're out there 'cause you didn't try out for (or didn't make) the football team. . .

Since their latest return from Europe the four have chosen to cool off the inevitable claustrophobia of being a single social and musical entity by temporarily splitting in their own directions. Klaus has put together an LP called "Shortnin Bread" on his own, while Ray and Biafra have collaborated on "The Witch Trials," a bizarre, slow-paced EP. As of this writing the DKs are on at least five compilation albums, most recently "Rat Music for Rat People," "Let Them Eat Jellybeans," and "Not So Quiet on the Western Front." And another LP, the most musically sophisticated yet, has been released on Alternative Tentacles—"Plastic Surgery Disasters." The lyric sheet you get with it is a deluxe insert of collages by Winston Smith, editor of *Fallout* and radical artistic mentor of the DKs. The statement Biafra made over two years ago to *Fallout* on the occasion of "Fresh Fruit"'s release applies in spades to "Plastic Surgery": "During the 60s Dylan and other artists did protest songs with acoustic guitar. We're just the modern equivalent—only LOUDER so more people will hear us."

Loud it is, but less frenzied than "In God We Trust." Here the message is drummed in more gravely, sometimes in cadences almost stately. Should you still be failing to get it, the insert urges you to write for further lyrics to Faulty Products in L.A. The sound is robust and meaty—couldn't be less like the faint hearts of our New Romantics. The reminders of early 60s surf music and TV themes are everywhere. And look at these rhyme schemes—Yeats invented "consonantal" rhyme, which paired "death"/"faith" or "turn"/"born," for example, but Biafra's using "vowellian" rhyme or something— rhythm rhyme:

I go to college   *John Belushi's my hero*
That makes me so cool   *I lampoon and ape him*
I live in a dorm   *My news of the world*
And show off by the pool   *Comes from* Sports Illustrated

I join the right clubs   *I'm proud of my trophies*
Just to build an impression   *Like my empty beer cans*
I block out thinking   *Stacked in rows up the wall*
It won't get me ahead   *To impress all my friends*

My ambition in life   *I want a wife with tits*
Is to look good on paper   *Who just smiles all the time*
All I want is a slot   *In my centerfold world*
In some big corporation   *Filled with Springsteen and wine...*

(*Terminal Preppie,* words and music by Biafra, © 1982 Decay Music BMI)

As for the future, who can say. By the time you read this the band may be dead or merely legend; Biafra may have gone back to his roots (drama school); Ray might have married his high-school sweetheart and moved back to Castro Valley; Klaus might have a hit underground radio show in Italy; Peligro might be drumming with. . . As successive wavelets of new thrash bands pound the headlands of Punk, obliterating all trace of what their ancestors inscribed in sand, the DKs' base of popularity is moving inland, toward the suburbs and the myriad "second" and "third" cities of America. (The same progression holds true for new wave as a whole.)

Not all bands go on to "bigger and better things." Especially ones that would rather be good than rich, rather be "interesting" than popular. Of course, being true to yourself *occasionally* pays off—but only occasionally. There is also the ever-present danger of burn-out, referred to by Miss Jennifer Waters after a gig that rather disappointed her:

To be fair, Biafra himself says there are good DKs shows and bad DKs shows, and now I know what he means. Not every night after four or five years can be a moving original experience. Maybe it's time to roll over Beethoven.

(*Ego* #4, August 1982)

Two things are sure, though: one is that it won't be drug problems that burn out this band, and the other is that the pendulum of social consciousness is swinging back toward politics again. Just a short time ago a second Congressional panel of inquiry concluded that JFK was indeed assassinated by some conspiracy unknown. Who knows? Maybe a bunch of kids born in 1963 will crack that case at last. "Leadership" won't always be an uncool concept, you know.

I make no other predictions. But it's simply impossible that the Dead Kennedys' spirit won't end up affecting quite a few kids even as it tears in one ear and out the other. And some of their music will prove pretty hard to forget, too.

© Lynda Burdick 1983

ROCK AGAINST REAGAN

© Winston Smith 1983

I am Emperor Ronald Reagan
Born again with fascist cravings
Still, you make me president

Human rights will soon go 'way
I am now your Shah today
Now I command all of you
Now, you're gonna pray in school
I'll make sure they're christian too

California Uber alles
Uber alles California

Klu Klux Klan will control you
Still, you think it's natural
Nigger knocking for the master race
Still you wear a happy face

You closed your eyes, can't happen here
Alexander Haig is near
Vietnam won't come back you say
Join the army or you will pay

California Uber alles
Uber alles California

(*We've Got A Bigger Problem Now*, words and music by Biafra, Greenaway, Ray, Flouride, Peligro, © 1981 Decay Music)

"Mowing down the people"

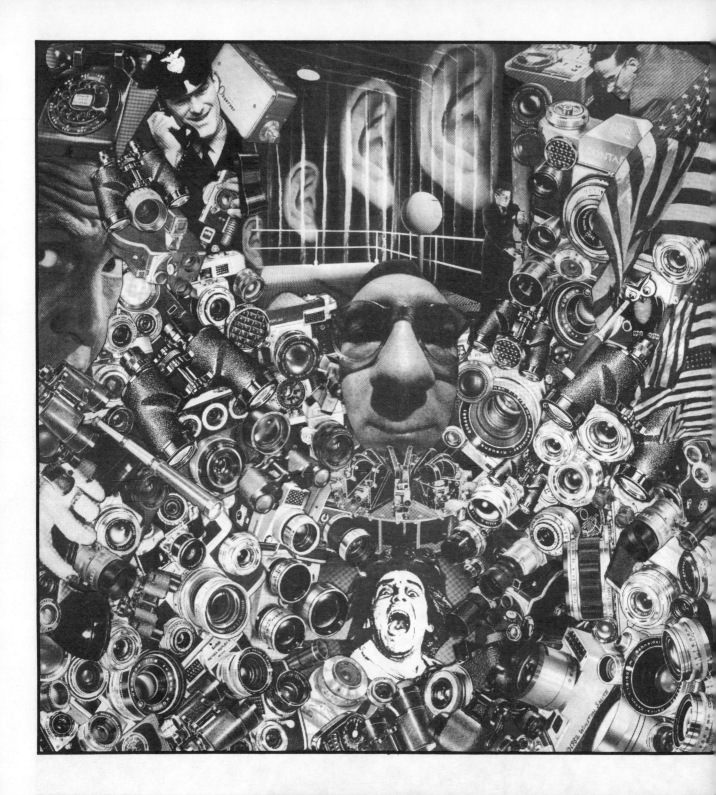

I AM THE OWL
I SEEK OUT THE FOWL

(*I Am The Owl*, words and music by Biafra, Ray, Peligro, Flouride, © 1982 Decay Music)

Vancouver Sun:
Isn't a Dead Kennedys concert on Nov. 22 in bad taste?

Ray:
Of course it is in bad taste.
But the assassinations weren't too tasteful either.

(November 22, 1979)

© Laura Levine 1983

GOVERNMENT BY GUNPLAY

On November 22, 1983, twenty years will have passed since John F. Kennedy was shot dead as he passed through Dealey Plaza in Dallas. Will that city see fit to mark the anniversary this year; for the first time, or will the task of remembering once again be left to diehard "assassination buffs"?

If what has happened since 1963 in America means anything, it is that *social amnesia,* the fatal forgetfulness of a people who take their "sovereign rights" for granted, is a most mortal enemy. Writing way back in 1964, Thomas Buchanan (quoted earlier) already seemed to know what the stakes were now that Kennedy had been murdered: they were nothing less than the good conscience of an entire society. Back then the irrational undertow that distorts our shaky modern lives, the shifting sand of lies that forms the bedrock of our smug nihilism, had not yet become chronic, and Buchanan could feel confident, in that far-off innocence, that the truth would yet have its say.

That he was wrong typifies our present malaise, a malaise that didn't begin in Dallas but was sent into a crazy spin there, a spin we may never snap out of. This nausea isn't confined to the U.S., either. A recent Hungarian film, "Time Stands Still," also fixes the year time stood still in Hungary as 1963 (not 1956); in one scene while the two protagonists are being rousted out of bed by their mother we even hear the news of Kennedy's assassination crackling over Magyar radio.

Young people in the mid-seventies had this sense that pop culture had been shot out from under them, that we had really been left stranded. That just before we came on the scene, all this really wonderful stuff had been going on, and what happened? All of a sudden everything swung back to normal and there we were on a desert island.
(Tom Carson interviewed by Michael Goldberg, *S.F. Examiner,* 4/4/82)

If we do break free of this out-of-control trajectory, it will be because some new "really wonderful stuff"—ideas, aesthetics, civility—gets invented by young and not-so-young people who haven't forgotten what it takes.

DISCOGRAPHY

Darren Peligro on drums for all 1981 releases and after;
Bruce Slesinger on drums for 1979 & 1980 releases.

7" 45s

California Uber Alles
Man with the Dogs (1979)
Alternative Tentacles (USA); 95x41
Optional Music (USA); Opt 29
Fast (UK); F12

Holiday in Cambodia
Police Truck (1980)
Optional Music (USA); Opt 4 (first 3000)
International Record Syndicate (IRS)
(USA); IR 9016
Cherry Red (UK); Cherry 13

Kill The Poor/Insight (1980)
Cherry Red (UK); Cherry 16

Too Drunk To Fuck
The Prey (1981)
Alternative Tentacles/IRS
(USA); Virus 2
Cherry Red (UK); Red 24

Nazi Punks Fuck Off
Moral Majority (1981)
Alternative Tentacles/Subterranean
(USA); Sub 24/Virus 6

Bleed For Me
Life Sentence (1982)
Alternative Tentacles/Faulty Products
(USA); Virus 23
Statik (UK); Statik 22

Halloween
Saturday Night Holocaust (1982)
Alternative Tentacles/Faulty Products
(USA); Virus 28

Nazi Punks Fuck Off
Flexi-disc in *Take It!* Magazine
March 1982

12" 45s

Holiday in Cambodia (1980)
Cherry Red (UK); 12 Cherry Red 13

Too Drunk To Fuck (1981)
Cherry Red (UK); 12 Cherry Red 24

Bleed for Me
Life Sentence (1982)
Alternative Tentacles/Faulty Products
(USA); Virus 23/12
Statik/Alternative Tentacles (UK);
Statik 2212/Virus 23/12

12" EPs

In God We Trust (1981)
Alternative Tentacles/Faulty Products (USA); Virus 5
Statik (UK); EP2

LPs

Fresh Fruit for Rotting Vegetables (1980)
IRS (USA); SP 70014
Cherry Red (UK); B Red 10

Plastic Surgery Disasters (1982)
Alternative Tentacles/Faulty Products (USA); Virus 27
Alternative Tentacles/Statik (UK); Virus 27

Compilations with DK Contributions

Can You Hear Me—
Music From the Deaf Club (1980)
Optional/Walking Dead (USA); OPT-LP-001
cuts: *Police Truck, Short Songs, Straight As*
(Bruce Slesinger on drums, 6025 on guitar)

Let Them Eat Jelly Beans (1981)
Alternative Tentacles (USA); Virus 4
cut: *Nazi Punks Fuck Off*

Not So Quiet On The Western Front (1981)
Alternative Tentacles/Faulty Products (USA); Virus 14
cut: *A Child & His Lawn Mower*

Rat Music for Rat People (1982)
Go Records (USA); Go 003
cuts: *Forward to Death/I Am The Owl*

Wargasm (1982)
Pax (UK); Pax 4
cut: *Kinky Sex*

Independent Projects

The Witch Trials (1981) EP
Subterranean/Alternative Tentacles (USA); Sub 17/Virus 3
A mysterious project with no musician credits on the album, but Jello and
Ray masterminded the project, Darren and Klaus contributed.

Shortnin Bread/The Drowning Cowboy (1982) 12" 45
Alternative Tentacles (USA); Virus 12
Klaus' solo project